FIDEL CASTRO

One of The Most Prominent Communist Leaders

THE HISTORY HOUR

HISTORY

CONTENTS

❦ I ❧
INTRODUCTION

"Men do not shape destiny; Destiny produces the man for the hour."

— FIDEL CASTRO

❦

Over the past century, Fidel Castro has emerged as one of the most prominent communist leaders. Fidel Castro ruled the country of Cuba for almost 60 years, and he changed the political structure of the country to a one-party socialist state. He ruled firstly as a Prime Minister before converting it to the title of President and Commander-in-Chief of Cuba.

❦

Castro's political journey started on a rebellious note as he participated in the revolt against right-wing administrations in Colombia and the Dominican Republic. He later rose to become the leader of the communist revolution.

❧

Within the span of Castro's career, he advanced from being a '***political illiterate***' to being a '***pro politician***.' With the aid of his anti-imperialistic politics, he was able to overthrow the then Cuban president Fulgencio Batista who had hitherto been backed by the US government.

❧

This book is a biography of the great leader Castro. In this book, we would highlight his strengths, weaknesses, mistakes and other attributes of interest. I hope you find this book interesting and inspiring enough to awaken the giant in you to achieve greatness.

❈ II ❈
THE UNVEILING OF
A HERO

"A revolution is a struggle to the death between the future and the past."

— FIDEL CASTRO

CHILDHOOD & EARLY LIFE

✿

Castro was born in Birán on August 13, 1926, a tiny town in eastern Cuba. His daddy was a rich Spanish sugarcane farmer who first emerged to the country through the Cuban Conflict of Freedom (1895-1898); his mom was a local maid for his father's family who gave birth to him out of wedlock.

✿

Castro's father being a rich man guaranteed Fidel a rich childhood home, but culture was clearly lacking - it was once described as "***barbaric beyond belief***" by a visitor. Perhaps this was the premise where he caught the resentment against America that became so important in his life. The revolution started inside of him while he was young. He was raised in the shadow of the massive sugar plantations owned by the US. His father once served in the army that warred against the Americans in the Spanish-American war of 1898. The defeat to Spain caused Cuba to be under US governance which caused disaffection amongst most citizens because of the US staunch support for out of favor dictators.

❧

Very few Cubans knew about Fidel's personal life. He met Mirta Díaz-Balart who he married in 1949, and she gave birth to his first son, Fidelito before they divorced five years later. He then had another companion who bore him five more sons. Fidel had other children from Naty Revuelta, who was a public figure, as a result of a romantic relationship.

❧

Fidel Castro was sent to live with his teacher in Santiago de Cuba while he was six years old. There he attended various schools before enrolling at the El Colegio de Belen in Havana. Fidel spent 11 years studying in boarding schools with seven years of it spent in Jesuits, where he had learned strong intellectual discipline. His best subjects as a student were history and geography. Castro was not an excellent student in academics, but he compensated the same in the field of sports as he played for the school's baseball team. In 1943 he emerged as the best secondary school athlete in the country.

❧

Action point

- Your background doesn't define you.

- Rise above your background to achieve greatness.
- If education is expensive try ignorance.
- Do your best wherever you find yourself and in whatever you do.

❧ III ❧
A LONG ROAD TO POLITICAL RECOGNITION

"Condemn me. It does not matter. History will absolve me."

— FIDEL CASTRO

POLITICAL PURSUITS

❦

fter leaving college, he preceded to the law school in the University of Havana where he got indoctrinated into the Cuban politics and nationalism.

❦

He joined the University Committee opposed to the US intervention in the Caribbean and struggled for Puerto Rico's independence. Castro chose the path of honesty, decency, and justice as he opposed corruption and openly criticized the US interference.

❦

After college, he traveled throughout Latin-America, taking part in rebellions in the Dominican Republic and Colombia. His vacations and political activities pressed him further towards Socialist ideas through before attaining power, he spoke about reaching his goals through democratic methods.

⚜

Castro soon rose to prominence among the freedom fighters, and he spoke extensively on the corruption and violence that characterized Grau's regime.

⚜

Castro took a step into politics proper when he joined the Cuban People Party in 1947. The party was a socialist group led by presidential candidate Chibas with the aim of attaining political freedom, economic independence and leading an honest government.

⚜

Castro headed the group which invaded the Dominican Republic in a bid to overthrow its right-wing president, who happened to be a close ally of the US. Though the attack was subsequently repelled by the US and Dominican forces, but Castro managed to escape the mass arrest.

⚜

The attempted mission did further to strengthen Castro's opposition to the Grau administration. Towards the end of the 1940s, Castro got exposure to Marxism and was profoundly influenced by its philosophy.

⚜

Castro soon found out that the problem of his country is not only the corrupt politicians but also the imperialist capitalist aided by the dictator. He also made a tour to Havana's most impoverished villages where he witnessed the height of social and racial inequalities. All these scenarios further strengthen Castro's resolve to become more active and radical in the University Committee's Struggle against Racial Discrimination.

ﻬ

Castro started his legal practice soon after graduation from the law school in 1950. He formed a legal partnership with Rafael Resende and Jorge Azpiazu dedicating more of his time serving as a human right advocate for poor Cubans whose right have been trampled upon. However, due to poor finances, the law firm was closed down. At this point, Castro knew his next destination is to delve into politics proper, and he joined the Cuban Peace Committee as an active member. After the death of the then ruler "***Chibas***," most people had seen Castro as the anointed candidate to take up the mantle of leadership in Cuba.

ﻬ

But instead, general Fulgencio Batista returned to power and canceled the scheduled presidential elections he set himself up as a dictator. This was made possible by the US government backing as well as the military and Cuban elite.

ﻬ

Castro was taken aback by this act of impunity that he made plans overthrow the government. So, he took along with him

140 loyalists with whom they attacked the Moncada military barracks in a desperate effort to overthrow Batista. However, the plan failed to yield a positive outcome as Castro was arrested, tried and imprisoned. However, this incident caused Castro's popularity to soar amongst the Cubans.

❧

Revolution is the struggle between the future and the past.

❧

Though in jail, Castro remained in touch with his revolutionary movement as he managed to keep the rebellious sentiments alive. In the meantime, Batista conducted the presidential election in 1954, but in the absence of any opponent, he was declared a winner.

❧

On May 15, 1955, which was two years after his incarceration, he was finally released. Working alongside his Mexican friend Ernesto "*Che*" Guevara, he perfected a plan to overthrow the Batista government. They both came up with a new strategy known as guerrilla warfare.

❧

The preceding year, Castro's band launched an attack on the government forces but failed like earlier. Castro fled with his brother Raul and friend Guevara to the south-eastern coast.

❧

Afterward, Castro formed a parallel government and started coordinating resistance groups in towns and cities across Cuba. Some agricultural reforms were enforced as he controlled provinces practicing agriculture and manufacturing.

❧

The military campaign was launched in 1958 throughout the critical areas in Cuba, which led to the government collapse and Batista fled to the Dominican Republic.

❧

Castro was lauded as a national hero. Castro became the commander-in-chief of the military while the Prime Minister was Jose Miro Cardona. However, due to Miro's sudden resignation, Castro became Cuba's Prime Minister on February 16, 1959.

PRIME-MINISTERIAL YEARS

❦

Castro assumed the office of the Prime Minister with a clause that the Prime Minister's powers be increased.

❦

In his hay years as the Prime Minister, various reforms were launched by Castro resulting in the turning factories and plantations to government owned. This move was targeted as a way to halt the US economic control. But, the restructurings created hostility with the US towards Cuba.

❦

Castro's political strategies endeared him to the lower classes, labors, workers, peasants, and so on, but he was sternly opposed by the middle class which was comprised of professionals, doctors, and engineers. The divergent views of the

Castro's government led to professional migrating of masses to the US bringing about economic brain drain in Cuba.

❀✿❀

Much of his governance style and policies depicts that of the communist which is being practiced in the Soviet Union. The assumption he vehemently denied stating that he runs Marxist-type of governance.

❀✿❀

Action Point

- Your passion determines your action.
- Channel your energy to advance your passion.
- There is no height a man can't attain with boldness, resilience and the right mindset.

❧ IV ❧

THE MYSTERY THAT IS CUBA AND THE ENIGMA THAT IS CASTRO

"The people of Egypt are an intelligent people with a glorious history who left their mark on civilization."

— FIDEL CASTRO

❧

Castro was on a part regarded as a brutal dictator who jailed, maimed or eliminated political opponents, shut out media, took private properties and bastardized the Cuban economy. But to others, he was an enigmatic leader who overthrew a corrupt dictatorship which was in connivance with the U.S. crime bosses, brought literacy to about 98 percent of Cubans, ensured availability of free health services and provided a full year of paid maternity leave to every new mother.

❧

Castro is regarded as an enigma even for death as he survived over 600 attempts to assassinate him and 11 hostile US presidents.

࿇

In one of his interviews he said:

> *"If there was to be given an Olympic medal for surviving assassination attempts, I would win the gold medal."*

࿇

Castro waxed stronger as each decade goes by as he became one of the longest-ruling leaders of a country, though this didn't decrease the plots against him.

࿇

HERE ARE A FEW OF THE ODD ASSASSINATION ATTEMPTS AGAINST HIM

࿇

Exploding cigar: This idea was suggested by a New York police officer to introduce an explosive substance into his cigar with the hope of blowing off Castro's head.

࿇

Hair removal: This is another plan based on spurious claims that if he loses his facial hairs, he will appear weak and unfit to rule. It was thought of by Americans to poison has cigars or shoes with chemicals.

***

Poisoned milkshake: This almost took Castro's life, fortunately for him the poisoned ingredient which was supposed to be put into the drink got stuck in the refrigerator and was cut open when the assassin who pretended to be a waiter tried to remove it.

***

Femme fatale: One of Castro's concubines allegedly struck an agreement with the CIA to feed him poisoned capsules. It was hidden in her face cream, but they dissolved.

***

Poisoned wetsuit: During the Bay of Pigs invasion the CIA planned to introduce deadly spores and bacteria, but this plat was foiled.

***

Exploding shell: This attempt was made to plant an explosive device in a mollusk with the hope that Castro will get attracted to while driving scuba.

***

Another deathly cigar: A poisonous toxin called Botulin was planned to be filled into his cigar only for the hired double agent to chicken out of the deal.

***

LSD: This has to do with a subtle ploy to make him lose credibility and sanity amongst his people. The plan is to expose an LSD-like substance into a studio as he does an interview on the radio which would make him act weird and cause him to lose credibility among his people.

***

Before his death, he had announced his retirement from active political life with a vow to keep "***fighting like a soldier of ideas***" by writing his essays which he calls "***Battle of Ideas***" essays. His adversaries from the West promptly charged the Cubans on the benefits of liberty and emphasize its position on the trade embargo.

***

But who is this Castro and what are the political exploits that have pitted him against the West and US especially?

***

This is a question that many researchers and writers have written on, and it leaves more to be desired. For many Cubans in the left, even though it is operating just one-party state, and a tightly knitted system similar to those in the former Eastern bloc, it reflects a model of matchless resistance to imperialism, a unique model of present times.

***

Cuba has experienced several forms of destabilizing

campaigns more than any other country as their leader has also survived numerous assassination attempts by the CIA. These acts are known to precipitate into state-sponsored terrorism as we know it now.

۞

Castro's coming to power coincides with the beginning of US coordinated grand conspiracies such as sponsoring rebel groups like the Miami exiles; who are the rich who prefer to identify more with Miami than Havana.

۞

As at the time when Castro toppled the corrupt government and became the country's leader against the wishes of the US, the country was heavily strangulated economically which drove Cuba closer to the Soviet Union. The US-Cuba tensions reached its peak during the 1962 Cuban missile crisis which almost caused a nuclear war. Through it, all the enigma remained dedicated, resolute in defense of his socialist ideology and Cubans right to determine its national identity and destiny. The superpowers reached a compromise, and the missiles were returned to the USSR safely. The rest is history.

۞

There is no gainsaying that the Soviet Union was Cuba's savior during the Cold war. It is on this premise that as the Soviet Union crumbled in the 1990s, many observers and world leaders were celebrating the demise of Cuba. It never came to their notice that Castro, through these connections has established a reliable social system which comprises of a vibrant education and health sector.

✥

Although the demise of the Soviet Union did create a vacuum and economic crisis, however, this was addressed through reforms that introduced the tourism sector for foreign and private investment. This served as another channel of revenue generation as they also barter medics for oil with countries like Venezuela.

✥

Castro's conquest and rule in Cuba symbolize heroic conquest and resistance to imperialism. There are so much great lessons to learn from the mystery that is Cuba and the enigma that is Castro as we reflect on his efforts to build a different and better societal model.

✥

Action point

- Never give up!
- Whether you do good or bad you will have enemies, so stand for what you believe in.

❧ V ❧
LEADERSHIP AND RESILIENCE PANACHE TO SUCCESS

"Someday, the capitalist system will disappear in the United States, because no social class system has been eternal. One day, class societies will disappear."

— FIDEL CASTRO

❧

There are several leadership lessons one can learn from the great hero and enigmatic leader Fidel Castro.

METICULOUS PLANNING A HALLMARK OF A GREAT LEADER

❧

The fact that Castro experienced the conviction and the guts to operate against the US for many years speaks amount about his prowess and undoubtedly planning that finally led him to effectively unveiling socialist authorities in Cuba.

❦

Tips for professionals: Regardless of how big the duty is made for you, with a strong belief in yourself and proper planning you will achieve your goal. If the correct plan is set up, execution may happen with ease.

BE COMFORTABLE AND HAVE FAITH

❦

Often a lot of time is put in in planning and on the other hands, the real circumstance is different. Despite planning, Castro's first coup failed. But he didn't quit, and in his second guerilla effort, he became successful in overthrowing the Batista government in 1959.

❦

Tips for professionals: Uncertainties are destined to occur in the organization world. But an innovator must be strong enough to fight and produce awesome suggestions to beat the chances. Be confident, trust yourself, and you will be rewarded one day.

KNOW YOUR FOLLOWERS WELL

❧

Fidel Castro realized early enough that over time nobody could push an enormous mass to do one's will. Hence it is vital to comprehend what your followers or employee wishes and then provide them with the same.

❧

Tips for professionals: Professionals must recognize that authority includes a whole lot of responsibility as well which comprises, a supervisor being in charge of his team. It's important that an administrator connects along with his team well, is aware of them and therefore create a friendly workplace.

HAVE STRONG TRUST IN YOUR IDEAS AND BELIEFS

❧

Fidel Castro today was once vehemently condemned in his own country and by the United States. Eventually, he has been successful in his objective by changing Cuba into a socialist country. Apparently that it was strong beliefs and conviction, that he could move mountains.

❧

Tips for professionals: When you hold a high position, many

will attempt to question your values, condemn you for your faiths. You'll have enemies who'll try to yank you down. But, never bend from your values and beliefs. Once you think firmly in yourself, a period will come when people will begin to believe in you. Their success is yours; this will likely, in the end, lead to your success.

COMMUNICATION IS THE CENTRAL ELEMENT OF ANY VENTURE

❧

"Communism is designed for the people; Capitalism for the leaders."

❧

From his quotations, it's very apparent that Castro was a great orator. His words possessed the power to place the people to silence. Talk can mold the thoughts of a massive number of followers. Fidel Castro recognized it correctly.

❧

Tips for professionals: Professionals must get better at the communication at best, if not the energy or oration. The greater silver-tongued these are using their communicative prowess; more effect he'll have on his/her team. In the organization world, effective communication is the central element to get work done.

❧

While Castro is gone, his thoughts and values will continue steadily to condition our futures in the professional and the non-public life. Castro was right when he said:

"History will absolve me."

⚛

In his 20s, Castro made moves to liberate his country from the hold of an armed service dictatorship. Eventually, he was successful. As soon as in vitality, his single plan was to provide the Cuban people - and humanity through internationalist solidarity. What exactly are the people of teenagers languishing in poverty and ineptness under tyranny all over Africa and South America looking forward to Arising!

RESILIENCE

⚛

He remains a great motivation to the teenagers of the country that are disturbed by the ever-increasing degrees of poverty, greed, and problem. Fidel's conviction for a just population led him into organizing two efforts to overthrow the then armed service dictatorship of Fulgencio Batista, and he was eventually successful at the early age of 32.

⚛

Fidel disembarked from the Granma fishing boat with a rebel military of 87 men and surely got to the Sierra Maestra mountains with significantly less than twenty guerrillas. Through such activities, he is continuously on the inspire those doing work for an improved contemporary society but are few in amounts. He was never discouraged by the increased loss of combatants or the higher fire-power of Batista's military; he comprehended that what he needed on his area was the support of the public rather than bigger guns.

❧

Fidel demonstrates to us to be prepared. It had been through planning and dealing with the public that Fidel Castro could beat the U.S-trained troops who fought against Castro's reign in 1961 at the Bay of Pigs. Castro's doggedness and preparedness have hindered the U.S from militarily invading Cuba since that time.

❧

Unlike the primitive deposition tendencies that people see with African leaders, Fidel Castro and his authority never sought materials riches for themselves. They functioned hard to ensure that each Cuban had similar and unrestricted opportunities to attain what they humanly could. That's how Cuba could achieve unequaled successes in the domains of education, precautionary and curative health, sciences, gender and racial equality, casing and career among other areas of human development. All of this was achieved regardless of the existence of the very most brutal monetary, commercial and economic sanctions from the U.S that is set up for more than 50 years.

❧

From the life of Fidel, a lesson on resilience and being true to self is learned. Few countries may survive a blockade including the one that has been enforced on Cuba. Through resilience, Cuba hasn't only survived that blockade but has been able to mobilize depends upon into condemning this U.S hostility. Each year at the UN Assembly, almost all countries except the U.S and Israel vote from the blockade. Fifty-four years into the embargo, the U.S Leader Barack Obama accepted that its insurance policy got failed and he commenced the procedure of normalization of human relationships between your two countries. However, the blockade remains in effect.

❦

After the USSR fall, Cuba lost its closest trading ally, and the overall Cuban economy was grounded. Many countries discontinued Socialism; many Socialist political parties around the world slipped Marxism-Leninism as their philosophy, and many Marxists philosophers and political figure no more wanted to be determined with Socialism. However, Cuba's Socialism didn't fall with the fall of the wall. The United States instead varied and realigned its Socialist current economic climate by moving towards renewable energy, popular organic and natural farming, pharmaceutical, and biomedical technology and other niche categories that are today the envy of several.

❦

Out of the resilience and ideas, Socialist countries started out to rise ten years later in other neighboring countries such as Bolivia, Nicaragua, Venezuela, Ecuador and other parts of Latin America. Leftist government authorities also became intense in Argentina, Brazil, and other Latin American countries. All over Africa, the aging '**_Marxist_**' scholars were substituted by young Marxist revolutionaries whose ideas are not based on Russia rather on the guidelines of equality and success of humanity, precisely like Fidel Castro has.

৪৯৫

Action point

- A leader is made great with great followers.
- Resilience is a very key characteristic of a leader.
- If you want to be a revered leader, improve your communication skills.

❧ VI ❧

FROM A ROGUE NATION
TO A PEACEKEEPER

"I find capitalism repugnant. It is filthy, it is gross, it is alienating... because it causes war, hypocrisy and competition."

— FIDEL CASTRO

❦

Under the control of Castro, Cuba showed the world the vital lessons on giving and solidarity. Cuban colleges have awarded a large number of full scholarships to young ones from developing countries who are portioned their countries as doctors and other experts. Cuba didn't grant these scholarships since it is a wealthy country. Rather Cuba has a lower GDP than that of several developing countries.

❦

Cuban armies have fought alongside their African compatriots in their challenges against colonialism and imperialism. Cubans aided Mozambique, Ethiopia, Angola, Algeria, South Africa, Guinea-Bissau, and Namibia either in their difficulties for freedom or in their wars against exterior aggression. So that as Raul Castro once said, Cuba fought together with Africans and remaining not with caffeine or vitamins, but with your body bags of the heroic military. Cuba's internationalist insurance plan is unlike the U.S globalization coverage; Cuba didn't sacrifice its citizen for them to exploit and dominate others, but it does so to fulfill its internationalist work to humanity.

೮⅓೮

Western Sahara is still Africa's former colony up even today. Are African countries looking forward to Cubans to come and rescue them from the colonization of the Saharawi Arab Democratic Republic? Or will the African Union commission reports persuade Morocco to leave European Sahara? Haven't we learned anything from the sacrifices of the Cuban people?

೮⅓೮

Today, Cuba carries on with this internationalist practice, however now by sending humanitarian needs where needed. From hurricanes in Asia and the Americas to the problems of Ebola in Western world Africa, Cuban doctors will always be on the frontlines of fighting with each other and formulated with these disasters. While discussing the Haitian earthquake, one Haitian indicated his appreciation to the Cuban doctors by saying that

"After God, Fidel."

Fidel provided us with lessons on how to deal with today's emerging offenses like terrorism. Within the 1980s and the 1990's, terrorists from Miami (recognized by the CIA) tried out to damage Cuba's travel and leisure industry by destroying hotels, Cuban airplanes, and various places of economic interests, even using bio-terrorism on innocent civilians. Instead of terrorizing and alienate innocent civilians like the Kenyan administration does today, Fidel directed his security staff to infiltrate the opponent and unearth terror strategies before they took place. That is how celebrated Cuban anti-terrorist heroes, popularly known as the Cuban Five had become (These were caught in the U.S and given tough life sentences for espionage but were freed by Leader Obama in Dec 2014).

Throughout his life, Fidel has survived an enormous selection of assassination endeavors on his life and most detrimental still on his personality, but this didn't reduce his resolve. They told lies about his riches, but he extended living an honest life. They lied about real human privileges violations, but he sustained to supply the highest attainable human being privileges for his people. Even at his loss of life, conservative media is continuously on to desecrate his name by submitting lies concerning this great groundbreaking. Fidel has trained us to disregard the liars and detractors and instead soldier on and do what's right.

Action point

- Do what is right and when you know better do better.
- Show love to others despite your challenges.

❦ VII ❦

THE REVOLUTION AND CUBAN'S LIFE UNDER CASTRO

"There is nothing that compares to the Holocaust."

— FIDEL CASTRO

❧

Castro (1926-2016) introduced the first communist leadership in the western Hemisphere after leading an overthrow of the armed forces dictatorship of Fulgencio Batista in 1959. He ruled over Cuba for over five decades, until handing over to his younger sibling Ramos in 2008. Throughout that time, Castro's rule was successful in lowering illiteracy, stamping out racism and increasing public healthcare, but was generally criticized for stifling financial and political freedoms. Castro's Cuba also acquired an extremely antagonistic relationship with the United States-most notably leading to the invasion dubbed

'**Bay of Pigs**' and the Cuban Missile Turmoil. The two countries officially normalized relations in July 2015, closing a trade embargo that was set up since 1960, when U.S.-had businesses in Cuba were nationalized without payment. Castro was declared dead on November 25, 2016, at 90.

EARLY YEARS

❧

After joining several Jesuit schools which includes the Colegio de Belén, where he performed well at baseball. He later enrolled as a lawyer at the School of Havana. While there, he became considering politics, signing up for the anti-corruption Orthodox party and taking part in an aborted coup to oust the brutal Dominican Republic dictator Rafael Trujillo.

❧

Do you realize? As well as the Bay of Pigs invasion, America made several failed efforts on Fidel Castro's life, which includes the poisoning of his cigar.

❧

In 1950, Castro finished education from the University of Havana. Two years later, he contested for election into the Cuban House of Representative. The election never took place, however, because Batista seized power. Castro responded by planning for a popular uprising.

"From that minute on, I had formed a clear notion of the struggle in advance,"

he said in a 2006 "***spoken autobiography***."

CASTRO'S REVOLUTION BEGINS

❀

In July 1953, Castro headed about 120 men to attack the Moncada military garrisons in Santiago de Cuba. The coup failed, Castro was apprehended and sentenced to 15 years in jail, and a lot of his men were wiped out. The U.S.-supported Batista, seeking to improve his authoritarian image, consequently released Castro in 1955 within an over-all amnesty. Castro finished up in Mexico, where he stayed with Ernesto "***Che***" Guevara and plotted his comeback.

❀

The following 12 months, Castro and 81 other men sailed on the yacht "***Granma***" to the eastern shoreline of Cuba, where authorities' makes immediately ambushed them. The approximate survivors were 18 in number with Castro, his sibling Ramos and Guevara inclusive, they all hid in the Mountains in southeastern Cuba with almost no weaponry or supplies.

❀

Matching to Castro, the revolutionaries started out reorganizing with only two rifles, but by early on 1957 these were already appealing to recruits and receiving small fights against Rural Safeguard patrols.

"We'd remove the men in the front, attack the guts, and then ambush the trunk when it started out retreating, in the landscape we'd chosen,"

Castro said in his spoken autobiography. In 1958, Batista tried out to snuff out the uprising with an enormous offensive, filled with air pressure bombers and naval just offshore systems. The guerrillas presented their floor, launched a counterattack and wrested control from Batista on January 1, 1959. Castro found its way to Havana seven days later and soon had taken over as prime minister. At the same time, revolutionary tribunals started out trying and performing associates of the old routine for alleged warfare crimes.

CASTRO'S RULE

๛

In 1960, Castro nationalized all U.S.-held businesses, including petrol refineries, factories, and casinos. This prompted America to get rid of diplomatic relationships and impose a trade embargo that still stands today. In the meantime, on Apr 1961, about 1,400 Cuban exiles trained and funded by the CIA arrived nearby the Bay of Pigs with the purpose of overthrowing Castro. Their programs ended in catastrophe, however, partially just because the first influx of bombers overlooked their targets another air effect was called off. Finally, more than 100 exiles were wiped out, and almost everybody else was captured. In Dec 1962, Castro freed them in trade for medical items and baby food price about $52 million.

๛

Castro publicly announced himself a Marxist-Leninist in the past due 1961. By that point, Cuba was becoming more and more reliant on the Soviet Union for economic and armed forces support. In Oct 1962, America learned that nuclear missiles had been stationed there, just 90 MLS from Florida, leaving fears of a global War III. Following a 13-day standoff, Soviet head Nikita Khrushchev decided to take away the nukes resistant to the hopes of Castro, who was merely overlooked of the discussions. In exchange, U.S. Chief executive John F. Kennedy publicly consented never to reinvade Cuba and privately agreed to have American nuclear weaponry out of Turkey.

CUBAN LIFE UNDER CASTRO

෧෧

After taking over power, Castro abolished legal discrimination, helped bring electricity to the countryside, provided for full work and advanced the sources of education and healthcare, in part because they build new academic institutions and medical facilities. But he also sealed down opposition papers, jailed a large number of political competitors and made no move toward elections. Furthermore, he limited the quantity of land a person could own, abolished private business and presided over casing and consumer goods shortages. With politics and financial options so limited, thousands of Cubans, including vast numbers of experts and technicians, kept Cuba, often for America.

෧෧

From the 1960s to the 1980s, Fidel made provision of military and school funding to various leftist guerilla moves in Latin America and Africa. Nonetheless, relationships in numerous countries, with the noteworthy exception of America, commenced normalizing. Cuba's market foundered when the Soviet Union collapsed in the first 1990s and America expanded sanctions even more.

⚜

Castro led Cuba in a Communist trend which resulted in a profound change in the financial and political fortunes of the United States. Castro reorganized the overall economy on Marxist-Leninist concepts. He's lauded by many for promoting education, interpersonal prices, egalitarianism and taking a stand to '***US imperialism***.' He's also criticized by many for the suppression of dissent, insufficient democracy, and a worsening overall economy, which led many Cubans to flee the United States.

⚜

Action point

- You don't need numbers to achieve greatness, all you need is a dedicated few
- Stand up for what you believe in; success will surely come with consistency

❧ VIII ❧
1953 INSURRECTION AND
THE VITAL LESSONS

"Men do not shape destiny, Destiny produces the man for the hour."

— FIDEL CASTRO

❀

In 1953, he led a coup to unseat Fulgencio Batista's right-wing regime. But, the attack on Moncada Barracks failed woefully, and he was jailed for his contribution. His trial worked in his favor as it was used by Castro to form semi-propaganda when he made a four-hour conversation '***Record will absolve me***' – as he openly criticized the injustice of Batista's government.

❀

"I alert you; I am just starting! When there is in your hearts a

vestige of love for your country, love for humanity, love for justice, hear carefully. I understand that I am silenced for quite some time; I understand that the routine will attempt to suppress the reality by all possible means; I understand that you will see a conspiracy to bury me in oblivion. But my speech will never be stifled - it'll go up from my breasts even when I think most by themselves, and my center will give everything the flames that callous cowards refuse it"

(Excerpt from talk 1952)

⚜

He also offered five vital revolutionary points that have been:

- The reinstatement of the 1940 Cuban constitution.
- A reformation of land privileges.
- The proper of commercial personnel to a 30% show of company gains.
- The proper sugar staff to get 55% of company revenue.
- The confiscation of holdings of these found guilty of scams under earlier administrative powers.

⚜

While in jail he put together the "***26th of July Motion***" (MR-26-7) which turned out to be a report group for Marxist ideals.

⚜

When he got free from jail, he left for Mexico where he joined up with Che Guevara and his sibling Raul Castro to create a revolutionary movement, focused on the ideals of Marxism-Leninism. The group's mandate was to topple the 'Capitalist-Imperialist' government and substitute them with Communist authorities who would cater to the welfare of the regular person and peasants.

❧

Batista's dictatorship alienated him from the people, and in 1959, Castro was a respected personality in the Cuban trend which effectively overthrew Batista and resulted in Castro growing as the dominating military and politics head. On 16 Feb 1959, he was sworn in as Prime Minister of Cuba. On loan consolidation of electricity, Castro launched sweeping economic reforms - a well-planned Communist status, which would assure healthcare, a sweeping expansion of education and public services for many. Foreign buyers were prohibited from further international land possession. Land possession was limited, and around 200,000 peasants received land possession. However, he soon reneged on his assurances of democracy - stating elections weren't necessary because of the previously evident popular support. In Castro's vision, he was a democrat because he sensed he had a large number of folks on his aspect, but the opposition was made illegitimate and political competitors arrested.

FIDEL CASTRO IN WASHINGTON, US 1958

❧

In 1959, when Fidel visited the United States, he was quite

popular and had a lot of publicity. But, his marriage with the United States soon got toxic as US companies found themselves struggling to operate in Cuba.

❧

Facing sanctions from the united states and a collapsing overall economy, Castro aligned himself with the Soviet Union - who decided to buy Cuba's sugar creation. Castro got economic aid from the Soviet Union and subsequently became a keen supporter of Communism.

❧

> *"I am a Marxist-Leninist, and I am a Marxist-Leninist before last times of my entire life."*

❧

For the Soviet Union, Cuba was a strategically important location near the US.

❧

Castrol also later modified Marx's saying to state:

> *"We have a theoretical idea of the Revolution which is a dictatorship of the exploited up against the exploiters."*

COLD WARFARE TENSIONS

❧

At the level of the cold war, the United States was deeply alarmed insurance firms are near neighbor turn into a Soviet-allied Communist express. The United States responded by imposing monetary sanctions and sponsoring tries to assassinate Castro and overthrow Castro's reign. This preceded the 1961 Bay of Pigs invasion; the CIA and Cuban rebels marketed that. The attack was a military services disaster and humiliation to the United States and only dished up to reinforce Castro's position. To several Cubans, they see Castro as their hero and voice.

❧❧

In 1962, He allowed the Soviet Union to position nuclear warheads on Cuban soil. This provoked a diplomatic showdown as the United States were worried about having nuclear warheads changed so near its place. After tense discussions affecting UN Secretary-General U Thant, the turmoil was defused, and nuclear warheads weren't retained in Cuba. But, the knowledge strengthened the United States persistence to weaken or overthrow Castro. This politics apathy to Castro was heightened by up to million refugees who fled Cuba and Castro's routine to the area in the United States. Refugees from Cuba were mainly middle-class experts, such as doctors and technicians who were probably to oppose Castro's program.

INTERNAL DISSENT

❧❧

Furthermore, to promoting circumstances managed the overall economy, Castro also instigated a control of the press and stifled internal opposition, gave room for no political opposition, and incarceration of 'counter-revolutionaries' who intend to undermine his authority.

ஃ

In the late 1960s, Castro became relatively estranged from the Soviet Union, and he became the first choice of the Non-Aligned Motion. Though reliant on Soviet financial help, he also continued to be linked with the Soviet Union through the Warsaw Pact.

ஃ

Castro was a great believer in growing revolution across the world. He delivered Cuban soldiers to African countries, such as Anglo and Libya. He also gained the support of several Arab countries for breaking off relationships with Israel, in response to the Israel-Palestine discord.

ஃ

Through the 1980s, Castro experienced increased difficulties. The United States president Reagan had taken a hardline to Cuba, which resulted in a heightening of rhetoric between the two countries. Within the Soviet Union, the reforming Leader Gorbachev declared Perestroika and Glasnost - which included economic liberalization and political liberalization. This designed a drop-in support for Cuba. But, Castro didn't follow Gorbachev's business leaders and ever more cracked down on dissent. As the economic situation went downhill through the 1980s Castro's populism which he previously enjoyed after the revolution was ebbed away.

FALL OF SOVIET COMMUNISM

❧

In 1991, Russia and the Soviet Union dropped aside with the end of a one-party Communist rule. This resulted in Soviet help ceasing, which greatly affected the financial situation in Cuba as the overall economy was struggling anticipated to US sanctions in support of limited tourism.

❧

By 1992, the Cuban current economic climate had dropped by 40%, and severe rationing was set up. In response, Castro became more modest in working with 'Capitalist' countries and searched for ways to diversify the overall economy into travel, leisure, and biotechnology - striving to lessen the economies reliance on sugar.

❧

Castro tries to find new treaties with left-leaning Latin American countries, such as Venezuela and Bolivia. The partnership with Venezuela is proven of a mutual advantage as Cuba gained petrol imports in substitution for medical services. Castro's decision to reduce the hostility towards faith and the Catholic Chapel - he set up a visit by Pope John Paul II which resulted in improved relationships between the government and the Catholic Cathedral. But, still, plenty of individuals wanted to leave for the United States.

❧

Within the 1990s, Castro embraced environmentalism and desired to boost Cuba's environmental impact - something was successful. However, despite some endeavors at small amounts, Castro has prolonged his criticism of US-led hegemony, accusing the United States to be the most detrimental polluter in addition to a strong proponent of the anti-globalization movements.

※

In 2008, worsening health issues caused Castro at hand within the Presidency to his sibling Raul.

※

Castro has announced himself an atheist and has criticized the utilization of the Bible for anti-democratic ideas. However, he stated that Christianity has many democratic ideas.

> *"If people call me Religious, not from the standpoint of religious beliefs but from the standpoint of public perspective, I declare which I am a Religious."*

※

Fidel Castro is a favorite political hero in many expanding economies - Africa and Latin America for his notion of egalitarianism and anti-imperialism. However, he's greatly criticized in many European countries, especially the United States for his rejection of democracy and suppression of internal dissent. Within Cuba, he remains favored by a significant portion of the populace for his nationalism and selflessness. However, many middle-class Cubans have gone in aggravation at the monetary and political limits.

◌⁓◌

Since his old age and ill-health, Castro had not been involved in administration, but he was still one of the dominating personalities of Cuba. In 2015, Barack Obama said the United States would get started normalizing relationships with Cuba, resulting in the likelihood that the years of sanctions could be raised.

◌⁓◌

Fidel Castro was announced dead on November 25th, 2016. The reason for death had not been mentioned.

◌⁓◌

Action point

- People do change, but never allow the change to affect what you once stand for.
- Don't let power corrupt you always have people around you to give you honest opinions.

TIMELINE OF U.S.- CUBA RELATIONS

"The people respect and believe in men who fulfill their duty."

— FIDEL CASTRO

꧁꧂

The following are the timelines of the events that have happened to Cuba since its inception and some landmark events that have happened through its history.

꧁꧂

1492 Christopher Columbus arrived in Cuba Island and conquered it as Spain ruled Cuba for the next 400 years.

꧁꧂

1868-78 Cuban revolutionaries war for ten years to break away from Spanish rule. Spain maintains control but promises reforms.

❦

1895 another revolt broke out against the Spanish government as the second independence war commences.

❦

1898 The U.S. assisted Cuba to war against Spain after the U.S. battleship Maine was blown up in Havana harbor. Together they were able to defeat Spain in the Spanish-Cuban American War. Spain relinquishes total control of Cuba.

❦

1898-1902 A U.S. military government rules Cuba.

❦

1901 Cuba takes on a constitution that consists of a set of provisions known as the Platt Amendment. The amendment gives the U.S. the liberty to intervene in Cuban affairs.

❦

1902 Estrada Palma was elected as the first Cuban president.

❦

1903 The U.S. receives a permanent lease on Guantanamo Bay

based on the treaty with Cuba and commenced the building of a large naval base.

❦

1906 U.S. troops came back to Cuba, and a U.S. led government rules in Cuba until 1909.

❦

1933 Another rebel group led by Fulgencio Batista ("**Batista**") takes over the government.

❦

1934 A treaty was signed by the U.S. and Cuba to abolish the Platt Amendment. Cuba's International investments expand between the 1940s and 1950s.

❦

1959 Fidel Castro's revolutionist's overthrow of Batista's government and Castro becomes Cuba's ruler.

❦

1961 Fidel Castro announces that Cuba is officially a Communist country. Cuban exiles supported by the U.S. CIA raided Cuba at the Bay of Pigs but were defeated by Castro's army.

❦

1962 U.S. laid a trade embargo: Making it illegal for U.S. citizens to travel or do business with Cuba.

One of the most severe incidents that arose during the Cold War is the missile crisis. This incident occurred in October when the U.S. was tipped off about a secret plan by the Soviet Union to install missiles in Cuba. After several months of tension and hostilities, the Soviet Union backed down on its initial plan as it removed its missiles and destroyed the missile bases.

1976 A new constitution is adopted, and it institutes the Communist Party as the principal power in the government.

1980 About 125,000 Cubans emigrated to the US. This event is popularly called the Mariel boatlift because the Cuban port of Mariel was used as their exit from the country.

1991 The fall of the Soviet Union and its Communist government. Cuba economy was also affected as it lost its most important source of finance.

1993 Cuba introduces economic reforms which give room for some workers to own private businesses.

1994 After another massive movement into the United States, an agreement on immigration was reached between Cuba and the U.S. The terms of the agreement states that the U.S will allow at least 20,000 Cuban entries annually. In return, Cuba promises to put in more effort to curtail illegal departures.

⚜

1998 Pope John Paul II visits Cuba which is regarded as a remarkable historical event because Castro's government had earlier banished religious freedom in the 1960s.

⚜

1999 A six-year-old illegal immigrant was saved off the Florida coast. The event raised eyebrows about how the U.S should handle Cuban exiles; He was eventually handed over to his parent in 2000.

❧ X ❧

AUDACIOUS GUERRILLA LEADER WHO CONVERTED INTO AUTOCRATIC ONE-PARTY SOCIALIST

"Something must be done to save humanity! A better world is possible!"

— FIDEL CASTRO

❦

Castro audaciously seized power against all the odds in 1959 and significantly commanded a powerful personal following within and outside Cuba's borders. But during his over six-decade-long reign in office Castro transformed from a famous and enigmatic guerrilla leader into an old-fashioned auto-cratic leader who seems suited for another age.

❦

Towards the end of his life, Castro was condemned continuously by foreign governments and human rights groups and despised his former friends and supporters, including his daughter. Yet Castro survived as one of the most noteworthy revolutionary leaders of the 20th century.

৩✕৩

Castro is one of the most distinct world leaders with his trademark look and green uniform. He has a trademark beard which he has been grooming since his young and physically active days. He coined a slogan "***socialism or death***" which he repeats severally during his later years; this is the right caption for a diligent and resolute rebel turned statesman who reeled with the current of history when it suits him but has the guts to attack it when it doesn't favor him.

৩✕৩

Even after the U.S President Barack Obama made moves to re-establish diplomatic relations and lift the over fifty years of sanctions, in a deal brokered by Pope Francis in December 2014, Castro still had mistrust in the US. A few days after President Barack Obama's historic visit to Cuba in 2016, Castro wrote a disparaging letter criticizing the president stating that Cuba needed nothing from its longtime foe.

৩✕৩

Driven by a conviction about his fate to overthrow the corrupt dictatorship of Batista, he accomplished an amazing feat of leadership. A mix of discipline, bravery, a keen instinct for popular feeling, good fortune and absolute force of personality was too much for Batista's large army to cope with. Castro's victory raised the hope of all rebel movements with and beyond Latin America.

⚜

Dismissing the hagiography that highlights that revolution cannot diminish the heroics of Castro when, on November 24, 1956, he journeyed from the coast of Mexico on the Granma to Cuba. The Granma ideally designed to contain only eight people, yet 82 armed rebels were crowded on board. The vessel was destroyed when it stuck on the coast, and only 21 survived an early ambush.

⚜

Castro led the survivors into a forest-covered mountain called Sierra Maestra, among whom were Raúl (younger brother) and his friend Ernesto "*Che*" Guevara, the Argentine doctor who became an international revolutionary.

⚜

In two years, Batista's regime was grounded as Castro's progressively popular rebellion exploited the government's internal weaknesses, which led to its abandonment by its ally the US.

⚜

By January 1959, a bearded renegade was coasting to victory on a tank through the streets of Havana. At 32 years old he has brought Cuba to his feet.

⚜

That feat achieved accompanied with the US President John Kennedy's botched attempt to remove him in 1961 through the sponsored attack by the Cuban exiles at the Bay of Pigs further increased his popularity and raised public sympathy.

༺༻

To many left-leaning politicians, Castro's socialist experiment highlights the birth of a new era for developing nations.

༺༻

"After this war is over, a much bigger war will commence for me: the war that I am going to wage against [the US]. I am aware this is my true destiny."

TALE OF DAVID VS. GOLIATH

༺༻

Castro rose to limelight in the 1960s and 1970s through his strong personality and charisma. He was an important member of the independent movement; which depicts the story of David standing toe to toe with the imperial Goliath. The David in Castro with small followers but resolute and determined to rise above all odds and might against them. The US got obsessed by Castro's government due to the heightened fears of the cold war with the Soviet Union. They saw Castro as a direct and imminent threat to its regional control, and it led successive U.S administrations to keep finding means to eliminate Castro as they over exaggerated his capacity for mischief. This led the CIA to coordinate several attempts to assassinate or discredit him.

Castro himself wasn't tolerant to the US as he often maintained a complex and ambivalent attitude. Although he loves baseball, he usually perceives the United States as the aggressor nation. He never let off the US for their role in supporting the Batista regime. This standpoint, combined with his brand of socialism, made him lean towards Moscow. The pact was a marriage of convenience: Nikita Khrushchev and his successors swapped economic and military aid for using Cuba as a cat's paw in the cold war with the United States of America.

Though he operated under the Soviet umbrella, he was often of a divergent view with Moscow. Castro expanded his international ambitions by posting aid and military advisers to Latin America, Africa, the Middle East, and the Caribbean to support governments and rebel movements. Perhaps he felt inhibited within the boundaries of a small island of with merely 11 million citizens; he had to export his revolutionary idea to make it safe at home.

His most daring and operational move was drafting troops to Angola in 1976 to strengthen the new Soviet-backed leftwing government. By the mid-1980s, the number has increased to over 50,000 strong force, which was later withdrawn after a ceasefire deal brokered by the US.

Cuba's desperate need for fuel was solved through their alliance with Moscow, and it also opened another new market for its sugar crop, which had been previously bought by the US.

⚜

The offer of soft loans and high support prices for sugar gave more room for development in the health, housing and education sector which was Castro's proudest achievement. Although this also came at a price as it put Cuba in a single-crop economy and associated it with distant trading partners with which they don't share the same ideals.

⚜

This deficiency came to bare after the cold war. Cuba was grounded by the collapse of the Soviet Union, where they had realized over $65bn in financial aid over three decades. The economy was in meltdown by 50 percent within four years from 1989, leading to a deep recession.

⚜

Initially, Castro refused to come into a realization of this fact and the need for a change in the centrally controlled economy — but in the span of time, his government appeared increasingly vulnerable to the social and economic forces besetting it. As economic conditioned deteriorated, he bowed to circumstance. In doing so, he reversed some of the major principles of his first three decades in power.

⚜

He started negotiating in a bid to attract foreign investment, allowed the use of US dollar for transactions, and legalized the private sector activities.

⚛

He also made agricultural reforms and tacitly caused unemployment when he shut down moribund state enterprises. However, all these reforms were only short-lived as he later gradually reversed some of these changes as economic situations got better.

⚛

His economic legacy was very clear: for all its social imbalances, the economy he took over from had a prosperous middle class and had one of the most beautiful infrastructures in Latin America. But his policies brought economic hardship, food allocation, and forced about 1.5m people into exile.

⚛

Action point

- Always leave when the ovation is loudest.
- Whatever you do today will become a history tomorrow so what the legacy you leave.

❧ XI ❧
PERSONAL QUALITIES
OF CASTRO

"Homeland or death! Socialism or death! We shall overcome!"

— FIDEL CASTRO

❧

Castro led the first revolution in Latin America to successfully defeat the military. Castro showed that he is a competent military strategist and an astute politician. The 1959 Cuban revolution was the largest popular support of any political movement in Cuban history.

❧

The revolution was based on a populist wish which made it

swiftly return to constitutional rule as it wrestled power from Batista government.

⚜

Once in control, Castro showed that he's a motivational and persuasive speaker who had the affection and support of his people. He was the deciding factor in redefining the future course of the revolution.

⚜

Over three decades he has endured in the limelight. Scholars, loyalists, analysts, and foes agree on at least one characteristic of the Cuban Revolution: Castro has been the undisputed political and ideological leader. It is true that vital policies mostly depend on what he chooses. He appears to be at the focal point of politics and economy, but he has to work within a certain framework.

⚜

Let's assume this is the case; it is essential to highlight some of the qualities of the man as a political player.

⚜

What are the features of the enigmatic leader Fidel Castro?

PERSONAL QUALITIES OF CASTRO

⚜

Castro is an active and pragmatic leader, a very decisive leader who takes action even if the action is a dangerous one. One can trace such character to his early childhood and his resolute character, persistence, and determination. He claims the motivation for is a revolution is all about struggle.

⚜

Castro is a dedicated person that loves to be challenged. He was referred to as an "***indomitable impetuosity***" one who doesn't give up by one of his teachers in the Jesuit College.

⚜

He is a disciplinarian who won't expect you to do what he won't personally do. He has a high self-assurance, and through his years on earth, he had only shown doubts on two occasions. Firstly, on the day, he arrived at Havana (January 8, 1959) when he was said to have asked one of his commanders; how am I doing? "***voy bien Camilo?***", Secondly on (July 26, 1970) when he decides to resign voluntarily. He projects a model of self-confidence to the public. His attribute of self-sufficiency adds to his overbearing frame of mind.

⚜

Resolute and self-assurance are both complimented by profound intelligence. Even opponents admit that Castro is intellectually sound, insightful, and well-read. Like most influential strategist he has a mysterious sense of timing. His loyalist and regard him as a man of integrity, selflessness, and personal courage.

⚜

His public speaking is well crafted as a person who thoroughly understands and exploits the psychology of Cubans. During his speeches, he educates, explains, persuades, instructs, criticizes, and attacks. He employs his oratory and public speech to inspire confidence, encourages collective reasoning and stirs to action. His speeches are in two dimensions as it combines style with content.

❧

The more you listen to his words the more it gains clarity, but it could be repetitive at times. Spoken words and public speaking has been one of Castro's forte as he showed this when he was freed from prison in 1955. This is one of the reasons why the Batista led government banned him from speaking in public but allowed him to publish his words.

❧

As earlier stated, while he was in college he loved history, and as he grew up in politics, he utilizes it as a weapon and a guide. In this century, he is the only Cuban politician who operates with historical examples, categories, and models. He has a weird sagacity of historical continuity.

DOMESTIC INFLUENCE

❧

Castro is regarded as a leader capable of sacrificing anything for him to remain in power. He used to claim that neither wealth, fame, quest for glory nor prestige motivates him. Rather, he claims that ideas are his motivating force.

***

Strangely, even though Castro has displayed the revolution's features, he doesn't have a clear and distinct philosophy or political thought. Although, there are a few ideas, core values, and policies which he emphasizes in his speeches. Indeed, he is a nationalist.

***

Fidel's unique influence has linked the defense of national independence with the need for socialism (done by 1961). This two-fold incorporation shows that the uprising and the nation are fused into one in his view. To survive a revolution, you need a revolutionary unity, which could be termed as national unity. If persuasion fails to yield the intended result, then the law, and the mass deployment of intolerance ensures unity through enforced public uniformity. In such a situation, neither political difference nor genuineness or honesty can flourish. Consequently, dissent, opposition, or questioning policies of revolution inevitably lead to a treason charge.

***

This revolutionary philosophy introduced by Castro can be summarized as: Collective needs are more important than individual rights.

***

- The motivating factor should be revolutionary consciousness not money just as selflessness is a seen as a positive value while greed a negative value.

- The state can make rational choices while the market is irrational, an emerging economy should be more focused with production rather than consumerism.
- Political needs come before economic prudence; a mass political contribution is more essential than a political choice.
- Unity is indispensable and loftier to divergent views, control of the center is more preferred to administrative independence.
- Mass mobilization is of better consequence than administrative methods.
- An accurate measure of democracy is the direct contact between a political leader and the populace, equality, and justice is more important than individual civil and political rights.

࿇

It is on these ideologies that key decisions have been made, and a new society created.

࿇

The Cuban political system that Castro built is an imbalance of formal institutions and charismatic authority. His leadership draws its powers not from the constitution but on the continual reaffirmation of his authority which he gets from the populace he was able to mobilize.

࿇

His close relationship with the population is where he wields his most power. This is the way he won widespread support and high regard in 1959 and has continued with this strategy since. From the mid-1970s to 1986, he ensured that institutionalization was allowed to thrive while his own very personal impeccable touch waned. But as the Soviet Union fell, the stability of his regime was threatened, and he went revert to the charismatic model.

◈

He then makes public the combination. This attribute shows Castro as a Great Communicator and a Great Synthesizer.

◈

As the enigmatic leader interacts directly with the public so do his people reciprocate by calling on him. They send him from all over the country numbering into thousands. It is interesting to note that a special team answerable to Fidel answers every letter sent to him. When all fails, there is Castro. Enigmatic authority is an arduous task.

◈

Yet, an enigmatic leader does not make decisions unilaterally. He has a "*support group*," an inner caucus which comprises of specialists who are knowledgeable and has earned Castro's trust.

◈

They must keep Castro well informed and updated of the latest events and happenings. They are expected to be savvy and hard-working. Over the years, the advisory group has evolved. The older revolutionaries have been succeeded by the university-educated.

❦

Castro holds several formal titles: First Secretary of the Communist Party, Commander-in-Chief of the Cuban Armed Forces, Maximum Leader of the Revolution, Chairman of the Council of State, President of the Republic, Chairman of the Council of Ministers, and member of the National Assembly.

❦

His greatest exploit is to have clung to power longer than any other Cuban ruler, notwithstanding the United States opposition. Domestically, he championed the radical transformation of Cuban politics, and economy; he also introduced a socialist system. His legality cannot be detached from the assistance that the population got through the policies of the regime.

❦

He championed the process of establishing new institutions. He introduced mass mobilization method regardless of the task. He also defined the arrangement of directing resources away from the urban areas and inspired his people to the belief that they have a fundamental right to a job, education and proper health care.

❦

Under his leadership, the revolution attempted to nationalize foreign property a feat that wasn't achieved in the Soviet Union.

However, some of Castro's notable shortcoming is the failure of Cuba to become more self-sufficient economically, its island economic inefficiency, and the over-dependence on sugar export.

Castro certainly had shown heroic, and wits in his exercise of power and have been willing to take high risks when he was sure that it would be a worthwhile risk to take to liberate his people.

FOREIGN POLICY

In the aspect of foreign policy, Castro's relationship with the US has been frosty from the onset. By 1960 the United States threw its weight behind the coup against Castro, and in 1961 the United States organized and led exiled Cubans to invade Cuba but was repelled at the Bay of Pigs. This is the first victory for Castro against the American imperialism.

In retaliation The United States imposing an economic embargo on Cuba. The conflict was further heightened during the missile crisis in 1962 which brought the world to the periphery of war.

Castro also understood the importance of global foreign policy to escape the sanctions imposed upon it by the U.S. in response to this, Cuba formed ties with Asia and Africa. Additionally, Castro started playing a pivotal role in representing the interests of the Third World countries in several forums. Cuban representative/ambassadors were sent to various countries like Angola, Algeria, Ethiopia, Nicaragua, and so on.

❧❦❧

From the time the U.S. imposed the economic sanctions, Cuba formed a special relationship with the USSR. Fidel Castro played a crucial role in networking the two countries while his country secured beneficial terms of trade from the Soviets. This feat ensured that the relations with the United States turned increasingly sour.

❧❦❧

However, the relationship with USSR was severed as the Soviet Union was disintegrated thereby putting Cuba at the most trying times of Castro's rule.

❧❦❧

With little oil reserve, raw materials and other consumer goods, the population was confronted with the most severe austerity measures. And they were faced with the inevitable which is a recession. This was undoubtedly the greatest challenge Castro ever encountered.

❧❦❧

The role of Castro in the 20th century deserves recognition as he plays a vital role in the history of Cuba, Latin America, and Third World countries. He is a standard for revolutionary experiments, and he attempted to incorporate Cuban historical tradition with European revolutionary theory. He made significant contributions to revolutionary tactics and strategies while revealing a Third World viewpoint on world affairs.

๑๕๛

Action point

- A leader must stand for something, or he will fall for anything. What are you standing for?
- A leader must know how to find the way around every circumstance faced in life.

❧ XII ❧
STRENGTHS AND WEAKNESSES

❦

Fidel Castro is a man with unique strengths which he exhibited before his historic revolution in Cuba. Castro leadership traits exhibited an abundance of strengths.

STRENGTHS

❦

- Ability to articulate revolutionary ideas and win more followers to buy into the idea.
- Exceptional public speaking skills.
- A genuine passion for the cause to liberate his people
- Equality and a sense of belonging to every follower

- Resolute, bold and committed to the cause he believed in.

WEAKNESSES

৩৯৩

Like most human beings' power, corrupts and absolute power corrupts. Castro allowed power to get the better of him. After a few years at the helm of affairs, he became less tolerant to criticism and suggestion from his subordinates. He fires ministers who question his judgment and replace them with those who won't question his opinions. Media and opposition were suppressed as politicians and journalists would often be arrested or jailed for daring to criticize his government.

❧ XIII ☙

INTERESTING FACTS
AND SUMMARY ABOUT
FIDEL CASTRO'S LIFE

☙❦☙

The revolutionist Castro died on November 25, 2016. During his extended political career, he became an enigma and an international figure whose importance and controversy transcends what was usually expected from the leader of a small Caribbean island country. He was regarded as a socialism champion by his supporters and as an anti-imperialist who helped Cuba regains independence. Conversely, he was viewed as a dictator who trampled on the human rights of his people leading to a large emigration of Cubans, and the decline in the country's economy.

☙❦☙

Whichever side you choose to view Castro as, whether as a

hero or villain, you will find these interesting facts about him educative.

- The longest speech ever delivered at the UN was authored by Castro. The speech which lasted for 4 hours and 29 minutes was delivered on 26th September 1960 at the 872nd plenary session of the General Assembly.
- Castro was known as a workaholic who usually retires to bed at 3 or 4 a.m. He prefers meeting with foreign diplomats in the early hours of the day as a ploy to use it to his advantage during negotiations.
- The novelist Ernest Hemingway was Castro's favorite author who wrote a few of his famous work in Cuba.
- Castro's over 4-decade rule made him the third longest-serving head of state, after Queen Elizabeth II and the King of Thailand.
- Castro's rule outlasted 9 US presidents starting from Eisenhower to Clinton. For a great part of his reign, successive US presidents imposed various economic and financial sanctions.
- Castro didn't have interest in music but was keen about sports as he spent time in the gym to keep fit and exercise regularly.
- Fidel Castro's private life remains private, and only a few information about him is in the public domain. But it is believed that he had five wives and eleven children.
- Fidel Castro was named in the all-time most influential 100 personalities by Time Magazine.
- Castro usually chews his Cuban cigars until he stopped in 1985.

- As a young revolutionist, Castro groomed his iconic beard. To him it wasn't just the symbol of a guerrilla fighter; rather he had other reasons for keeping it. He believed that 15 minutes spent daily shaving will translate into 5,000 minutes a year which could be spent on other important activities.
- At the age of 21, he went to the Dominican Republic in 1947 to partake in the coup of Dictator Rafael Trujillo, which forms the foundation of his proclivity toward armed rebellion.
- One of Castro's cows, called Ubre Blanca (White Udder) was named in the Guinness Book of World Records for producing the highest milk yield in a day - 110 liters. Castro often made reference to this cow's astonishing yield in speeches to back up the claim that communism has higher breeding skills.
- Theodore Draper, an American historian, created the term "***Castroism***," which signifies the merger of Latin American revolutionary tradition with European socialism.
- Castro was interested in gastronomy, wine, and whiskey. He usually visits his kitchen to converse about cookery with his chefs.
- Castro formed a pact with the Soviet Union in the mid-1960 when the U.S. fired nuclear missiles in Turkey; this was because he regards it as U.S. threats against Cuba. He gave his consent for nuclear weapons to be placed in Cuba by the Soviet Union which later sparked a Cuban Missile Crisis which led to the Cold War.
- Castro's English was very fluent, but the rather prefers not to communicate in English both in

public and private domain as he considered it as his enemies' language.

- Fidel Castro was admired by many as well as some of the most popular American celebrities like Chevy Chase, Steven Spielberg, Kevin Costner, Robert Redford, Jack Nicholson, and Oliver Stone.
- Castro authored many quotes. Some of his famous quotes include,

"Revolution is not a road filled with roses. A revolution is a battle to the last drop of blood between the future and the past,"

and

"Men don't shape destiny. Destiny makes the man for the hour."

- Castro reversed his earlier stance about LGBT rights in Cuba. This came after his government had effectively persecuted and imprisoned homosexuals and cultural dissenters in the 1960's. In 2010, Castro expressed remorse over this policy. Mariela Castro who is Castro's niece is an LGBT activist currently speaking out for the right of lesbians in Cuba.
- Castro preferred dressing style for the most part of his reign is the military styled clothes, but in his last years, he embraced a more relaxed style. Particularly he wore sport brand Adidas jackets to important political meetings.
- Hugo Chavez, Castro's bosom friend, and closest political ally served as Venezuela's president from 1999 till 2013 when he died.

- Castro abdicated the Cuban presidency to his brother Raul in 2008 due to his ailing health.
- Fidel executed many restructurings designed to favor Cuba and not the United States, and this resulted in the US labeling him as a '***Communist***,' and '***dictator***.'
- As Cuba formed diplomatic relations with the Soviet Union, political relations with the U.S. deteriorated.
- Castro made his first attempt to overthrow the dictatorship regime of Fulgencio Batista's in 1953 but failed woefully as he was arrested and sentenced to 15 years. However, he became more famous through his arrest as he got recognition and public sympathy.
- He was imprisoned for two years as he benefitted from an amnesty deal in 1955. His marriage also crashed that year.
- He launched another plan to overthrow the government in 1956 after he had learned more about guerrilla warfare in Mexico when he visited Che Guevara. With 81 rebels they failed, and most were captured or killed. Castro escaped with his brother.
- At the third attempt, he got successful and took control of Cuba in 1959 becoming the commander in chief of Cuba and later the prime minister after Jose Miro Cardona resigned.
- Castro functioned as Cuba's Prime Minister between 1959-1976; afterward as Cuba's president between 1976 to 2008 till he stepped down and handed over to his brother due to health issues.

HOW CAN WE USE CASTRO'S STRENGTHS IN OUR LIVES?

⚜

Anyone aspiring for a leadership post should take a cue from this revolutionary leader and master his strengths while learning from his weakness.

⚜

Castro's strength can be applied to our lives through constant development and seeking knowledge. Leaders are made and not born. One should learn how to effectively communicate one's ideas to others in an inspiring way. Develop public speaking skills and learn how to pass on your ideas to others in a concise and articulate manner. Great leaders are often great orators; learn to be one. If you are working in a group, learn to give everyone an equal opportunity to excel. Let everyone have a sense of belonging then they can stay true and committed to the cause.

⚜

All through Castro's life, he showed incredible boldness and resolute even in the face of a lot of challenges. You should learn this also but ensure you are determined on the right premise, not on the wrong premise and always evaluate your performances, so you will know when you have derailed or not.

❧ XIV ❧
CONCLUSION

❧

While there are varying opinions about Fidel Castro throughout the world, no one can disagree that he showed an obvious ability of successful leadership. He started as a man with big dreams and with his firm, unwavering beliefs he garnered countless supporters who stood him through thick and thin to achieve what they considered best for the country. He was a man of influence who certainly made a difference and inspired others to help achieve worthy goals.

❦ XV ❧
FURTHER BOOKS
TO READ

❦❧

Below are further books to read for more information about the enigma called Fidel Castro.

- Title: My Life (Fidel Castro with Ignacio Ramonet)
- This is a spoken autobiography with over 100 hours of interviews about his early life, the early failures of his revolution, and his thoughts on the US. It's essentially a book you need to know more about Fidel.
- Title: Reminiscences of the Cuban Revolutionary War (Ernesto 'Che' Guevara)
- Che Guevara was Fidel's friend and medical doctor who provide an eyewitness account about Fidel Castro.

- The Man Who Invented Fidel: Herbert L. Matthews of the New York Times (Anthony De Palma)

This book helps to understand Castro's perspectives about governance.

YOUR FREE EBOOK!

As a way of saying thank you for reading our book, we're offering you a free copy of the below eBook.

Happy Reading!

Made in the USA
Columbia, SC
07 July 2020